W9-CDO-505

First Facts®

The Solar System

NASA

by Steve Kortenkamp

Consultant:
James Gerard
Aerospace Education Specialist, NASA
Kennedy Space Center, Florida

Capstone press®

Mankato, Minnesota

First Facts is published by Capstone Press,
151 Good Counsel Drive, P.O. Box 669, Mankato, Minnesota 56002.
www.capstonepress.com

Library of Congress Cataloging-in-Publication Data
Kortenkamp, Steve.
    NASA / by Steve Kortenkamp.
    p. cm. —(First facts. The solar system)
    Summary: "Describes the National Aeronautics and Space Administration, including its
development and accomplishments"—Provided by publisher.
    Includes bibliographical references and index.
    ISBN-13: 978-1-4296-0062-0 (hardcover)
    ISBN-10: 1-4296-0062-4 (hardcover)
    1. United States. National Aeronautics and Space Administration—Juvenile literature.
I. Title. II. Series.
TL521.312.K67 2008
629.40973—dc22   2006100079

Editorial Credits
Jennifer Besel, editor; Juliette Peters, set designer; Patrick D. Dentinger, book designer; Jo Miller,
    photo researcher

Photo Credits
Digital Vision, cover (shuttle and astronaut on moon)
Dreamstime/Instamatic, 20 (joystick); Joegough, 20 (detector)
Folio, Inc./NASA/Bill Ingalls, 6
Getty Images Inc./Hulton Archive/NASA, 16
NASA, cover (astronauts), 5 (top left and top right), 7, 9, 11, 21; Alan L. Bean, 13; JPL/Cornell
    University, 17; Kennedy Space Center, cover (control center), 5 (bottom), 14; Lockheed Martin
    Corporation, 18–19; Richard Clark, 1
PhotoDisc, cover (probe)

1 2 3 4 5 6 12 11 10 09 08 07

Table of Contents

Exploring NASA

Have you ever wanted to float around a space station or walk on the Moon? Would you like to help build the rockets that send astronauts into space? The people who do these jobs work for an agency called NASA.

NASA Headquarters, Washington, D.C.

What Is NASA?

NASA stands for the National **Aeronautics** and Space Administration. NASA is an agency that is part of the United States government.

Some people at NASA work to make airplanes safer. Others study space. They use telescopes and **space probes**. NASA astronauts explore space.

Where Is NASA?

NASA has workers all over the United States. They send up rockets in Florida, build space probes in California, and train astronauts in Texas.

But NASA's coolest workplace is in space! NASA astronauts work on the space station. Robot space probes built by NASA explore the solar system.

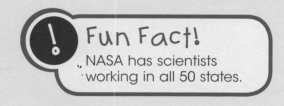

Fun Fact!
NASA has scientists working in all 50 states.

9

How NASA Started

In 1957, a space race between the United States and the **Soviet Union** began. Each country wanted to be the first to land people on the Moon. To help win the space race, the United States started NASA.

Fun Fact!
The first NASA astronaut went into space in 1961.

Exploring the Moon

The United States won the space race in 1969, when NASA astronauts walked on the Moon. But NASA's job wasn't done. They sent more astronauts to the Moon. Astronauts collected Moon rocks. They also left experiments there. Scientists on Earth study the rocks and experiments to learn more about the Moon.

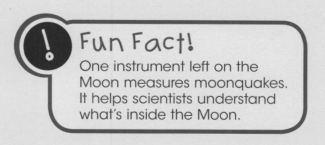

Fun Fact!
One instrument left on the Moon measures moonquakes. It helps scientists understand what's inside the Moon.

Space Shuttles

Astronauts going to the Moon had to use a new **spacecraft** every time they went into space. NASA wanted a spacecraft that could be reused many times. So NASA workers developed **space shuttles**. Space shuttles are sent up with rockets but land like airplanes.

! Fun Fact!
NASA built five space shuttles. These shuttles have carried hundreds of people into space and back to Earth.

NASA's Robots

NASA's space probes have explored every planet in our solar system. These probes gather information and take pictures for scientists on Earth.

Two of NASA's robot **rovers** have been on Mars for more than three years. The information they gather is used by scientists on Earth.

NASA's Plans

NASA has big plans for what they want to do next. Right now, NASA is building a new spacecraft named *Orion*. Astronauts will use *Orion* to return to the Moon and to practice for a mission to Mars.

Amazing but True!

Did you know that NASA helped make many of the things we use every day? NASA made better smoke detectors to alert astronauts to harmful gases on the first space station. And the joystick controllers you use for some video games were originally made to help land a rover on the Moon.

Think Big!

NASA is a very busy agency. There are people working on airplanes, rockets, space shuttles, and robot space probes. The person in charge of NASA gets to plan where all this technology can be used in new missions. If you were the one in charge of NASA, what new mission would you plan for the future?

Glossary

aeronautics (air-uh-NAW-tiks)—the science and practice of designing and building aircraft

rover (ROH-vur)—a small vehicle that people can move by using remote control; rovers are used to explore objects in space.

Soviet Union (SOH-vee-et YOON-yuhn)—a former group of 15 republics that included Russia, Ukraine, and other nations in eastern Europe and northern Asia

spacecraft (SPAYSS-kraft)—a vehicle that travels in space

space probe (SPAYSS PROHB)—an unmanned spacecraft that is used to explore space

space shuttle (SPAYSS SHUHT-uhl)—a spacecraft that is meant to carry astronauts into space and back to Earth

Read More

Burgan, Michael. *Spying and the Cold War.* Freestyle Express. On the Front Line. Chicago: Raintree, 2006.

Kerrod, Robin. *Dawn of the Space Age.* History of Space Exploration. Milwaukee: World Almanac, 2005.

McNeese, Tim. *The Space Race.* Cornerstones of Freedom. New York: Children's Press, 2003.

Internet Sites

FactHound offers a safe, fun way to find Internet sites related to this book. All of the sites on FactHound have been researched by our staff.

Here's how:
1. Visit *www.facthound.com*
2. Choose your grade level.
3. Type in this book ID **1429600624** for age-appropriate sites. You may also browse subjects by clicking on letters, or by clicking on pictures and words.
4. Click on the **Fetch It** button.

Facthound will fetch the best sites for you!

Index